The Woman
Who Tries to Believe

Barbara Daniels

ISBN 0-9636545-6-X

Acknowledgments

The author wishes to thank the editors of the following publications where these poems first appeared, some in slightly different form:

The Massachusetts Review: "This Is a Practice Planet," "The Woman Who Tries to Believe."
Four Quarters: "Just Looking," "The Ordinary Destination," and "Losing the Farm," recipient of the Richard E. Lautz prize from *Four Quarters.*
Footwork: Paterson Literary Review: "During the Prelude."
Thema and *Mirrors and Stars:* "The Circulation of the Blood."
Outerbridge: "I Stole Your Book."
Pegasus and *Mirrors and Stars:* "My Friend, Dead in a Winter Storm."

Forthcoming:

Slant: "A Sense of Direction."
Laurel Review: "Finding the Way Out."
Seattle Review: "The Mermaid and the Platypus."

Cover photographs:
    Front: James Baker Hall
    Back: Glenna L. Huls

Contents

To David

This Is a Practice Planet

On God's bruised lips he tastes the metallic flavors
of regret. For him we're like family, too much alike,
men especially, their size wrong for the spaces
next to cribs, their arms so high they must bend

cumbrously to lift wet dishes from the dish water.
God reaches for the reset button. He sees
the massive darkness, bursts of color and
the slow ticking over. This time he'll check

the systems. But regret stays his hand
in the humid air. A single finger, knuckle
swollen, points at nothing. Then God
folds his fingers into his armpits and leans

slightly toward us. He's fond of men, the way
they stand at altars in their white vestments,
the things in their hands—axes, dayplanners,
Nintendo games. He knows their desire

to wield an axe, use rage as a tool, heavy,
shining dully, thrown by a muscled arm. He knows
his face is red with grief. He wanted everyone
to act in the world, violet-green swallows knifing

through transparent spaces, spiders lifting
and dropping their own bodies, dogs systematically
patrolling lawns, women starting meetings,
calling them to order at the right time.

During the Prelude

By nine fifty I'm hunched in a pew, scrutinizing
the bulletin down to the names of the greeters who touch
each person at the main door and the other couple,

plopped in their seats like balloons filled with sand,
the ones who chose the altar flowers. They judge
their bouquet, compress their lips, and nod, finally, willing

to pay. God is motionless on these spring mornings.
The salaried organist flips to her last page. The choir steps off
from the back. I do not turn. I know the ministers

have synchronized their watches like referees before a swim meet,
slender, already suited up. Together, they pace to the front.
I sweat in my decent dress. My husband arrives at the lectern.

He is about to speak, the white tab in the center of his collar
plastic, cheaper to buy than cloth, cheaper to clean.
I study the nubs of stocking that pimple my ankles. My heart

is a heavy bag. Thick deposits form there, narrowing
the channels. If only I were holding the *New York Times*,
blackening my fingers, smearing my face with the ink.

Swaying

Maybe I have two souls, facing
in different directions. I don't know.
Is my spine like the softened bones
in a can of salmon, the cause
or effect of insufficiency?

My eye keeps twitching. Perhaps
there is a part of myself
that I could sell? Is there a bird
inside me? A mismanaged heart?
Is it wrong to wish for so little?

The tallest buildings move so gently
no one feels their easy swaying. I wish
the people I've loved were sleeping now,
on their backs, hardly dreaming,
unaware of the pitching and rolling

beneath them. I wish that woodstorks
stood around me, that I could see
their heavy bodies, hear them slip
their legs out of the water,
beat their way into the air.

Woman Howling

When the woman tells her friends
she has a rich inner life, she means
she goes to cheap motels in the afternoons.

In her pew at church a light seems to shine
on her yellow hair. Everyone knows her,
the minister's wife. She listens to the stories

other people tell of other women's men
and their moods. When she must walk
among the congregation, her body

is her disguise. She goes to the day school
of desire, a man with a red moustache.
Others had asked her, the meter reader,

sniffing her need, a high school boy
with curling hair. Alone at night,
she steps into a closet, closes the door.

A neighbor walks nearby, his little dog
nosing the neglected bushes. The man hears
the woman howling, knows what it says,

an inner life like a box of knives, like a dog
in a trap who chews till he bites the bone.
The woman thinks of gifts her lover brought her.

On the long ride home from the Elms Motel,
she stopped once, put roses in a culvert
under the road, near them a golden chain.

The Pruning

I wrote *long life* on the leaves of my orange tree,
peace and *luck* on the soles of my shoes.
On the pages of your books I wrote music, songs
for one hand at a piano, answers in oboes
and flutes. Rain and long walking smudged
my shoes, every step a prayer. White shirts
and spring dresses blazed in the parks.

Loosened ties said *respite*. *Warmth* lay down
on the bending grass. At home my orange tree
reached for the ceiling, touched and bent over
in its little room. I hate to prune
but I had to. I stood on a chair, pulled
the fragrant branches to me. *Leave me*
said my shining blade. *Cry out and fall away.*

Finding the Way Out

More women have done this
than you can imagine, driven cars
till they're out of gas, stepped
onto bare ground, walked

from field to field collecting stones,
slept in the blonde grass. I know
I could live like an animal, let
knives darken in their wooden cases,

dust thicken on smeared mahogany,
dishwater curdle in the cold sink.
I've got my story: It's a form
of getting out, a long flat highway

or a short escape—a dream
in the morning before the alarm.
Even a hummingbird falls asleep,
slows the constant motor of her heart,

lets trumpet flowers bloom
in her trembling eyes. Truly gone
is harder, but it can be done.
Women get away on a daily basis.

You just don't see them in the flagrant
rain, the solemn fog that starts the day.
They pick up their pocketbooks, open doors,
pin red flowers in their gleaming hair.

The Circulation of the Blood

In Dr. Wu's office a TV exhorts us
to cut fat, exercise, fight stress while a radio
begs us to love Jesus, turn to Him.

Large, sad bodies fill the narrow waiting room.
No one is listening. A stranger mashes
her wet Kleenex. "I was fine at the funeral,"

she tells us. "My daughter says to go out.
Getting out will help." "He's a fine doctor,
Dr. Wu," a man replies, turning stiffly

to the TV screen. I should have something
to give. I consider the contents
of my pocketbook—credit cards,

lemon drops, a book of skeptical poems.
I look at the spots that freckle my wide hands,
stains I will take to my grave.

On the wall, blood circulates through a closed
system, to the heart, away from the heart.
I turn the pages in my little book.

In Separate Cities

We all know what rhyme is.
—Mary Oliver

A child and her sister rhyme,
punching each other with thin fists.

The long route of butterflies rhymes
with a missing glacier their bodies remember.

Hollows in an owl's skull echo your own—
the delicate bones around your eyes.

The roses you brought me rhymed,
each with each in a blue jar.

Highways loop and repeat their yellow lines,
their broken white lines.

Flags still sigh to each other, rippled by winds
in every state, some unraveling, letting go.

My mother is lifting fallen pots.
She brings the brown bulbs home,

plants them in her narrow yard.
When they bloom again, she'll remember

their twisting and blurring on my father's grave.
In our separate cities, you and I rhyme,

each with each. Our steps pace out
alone past locked buildings, past

men and women, palms out, asking.
Their upturned hands rhyme with ours.

At the Mutter Museum

A baby's been swimming in a bottle
for a hundred years. Her large head tilts
inquisitively. Cord from her body
and her mother's body twists
around her, the bleached snake
that killed her and brought her here,
the oddity museum, to sit among shelves
of skulls, hearts, articulated bones.
My arm jolts her cabinet, stirs
the preservative, lifts her head
as if the eyes were opening, the little
mouth. Her hand taps the glass.

I've always listened for messages.
I lay on my bed, ten years old.
Down by the soybean mill a train whistled,
slid out of town to cornfields,
a long flat landscape. I wanted
to live in the body of a woman,
far from home. Everything
I learned then proved to be wrong.
The center of the earth is a crystal,
clear, like a diamond, a heavy stone.
I believed that it was liquid, molten lava,
that it moved like a living heart.

The Mermaid and the Platypus

A wizened monkey head, cut from her body, glued
to a fish, convinced. Men thought they held a mermaid
shipped from the China Sea. Trusting the evidence
cupped in his hands, one man whispered,
"I could teach you Greek." Then he dreamed
night after night that rounded weights
pulled him down in green water. Fighting up
through twisted hair, he woke, trembling.
Then the head, lifted once too often, fell away
from her half fish and rolled off a table.

No wonder no one believed in the platypus,
her blue-gray skin dried in a frill on her beak,
her velvet hair, smooth as a rabbit's.
Now we know. The platypus snaps
her eyes and ears shut and dives blind,
seeking and touching with her gentle mouth.
Captive, she dies, or if she lives, learns to stand
completely still, slowing her heartbeat,
while a man, her keeper, strokes
and strokes her soft, compliant bill.

The Sorrow of Trees

Giving birth to themselves, trees explode,
leave the burning pieces, ram blind,
tuberous faces up through packed dirt.

Young, they might be sticks, weeds.
Most die. To live, the rest must stiffen,
stand alone. Each new season brings a tight

little ring. New bark hurts like lumps
that turn into breasts on a child's chest.
Trees hate webs of pearled dew,

the yellow-green of new leaves,
the bitter effort, necessary weight.
The trees believe they could almost walk,

stump along like amputees. Laughter
slides uneasily through whistling leaves.
Their children grow around them,

grow and die. Grit and sand grind
against their arms, their hands.
Every gesture hurts. The cries

from aging trees are real. "I can't
remember bending," they complain.
They cannot name the year, the day,

the president. "This man claims
to be my husband," one tree says.
"Who is he? Who are all of you?"

Teaching the Comma

Commas gather in sentences like tree swallows
perched on telephone lines. They lift
their metallic wings in the bright air, arc out,
cut back, and settle on the looping wires.
Without commas, who could remember to breathe?
(the ache of expanding the chest, the ache
of compressing the chest)

I mark each comma in my Hammett's No. 516
Class Record Book. But commas are so often late,
so often inattentive. Or they sit, separately,
in the darkened classroom,
waiting again for my late arrival.

Take this. Learn the comma.
It is bread for you.

I might as well be bleeding, I am bleeding,
from my nose, my ears, my mouth. Blood drops
on my dress like crushed berries from a tipped bowl.

I stumble out and fall where glass doors open
onto agitated leaves. These green leaves
struggle in the moving blades of light.
Bells ring. The classes change. A student comes
to wash me with brown paper towels.
She holds my wet head in her sticky arms.

Men from the school gather in the doorway,
smell the blood. Men from the rescue squad
touch me, turn me, talk together, drive away.
Quiet light from their ambulance spreads
through the trees full of flowers.

At the end I lie still, small
in the angle between the floor and the wall,
and say again the rules for commas.

I Stole Your Book

My hand went out to the book you left
in Room 301 and it was mine. I took
what I wanted the way I stole a man once,
a boy really, told myself it didn't matter,
then cried in his bathroom
with the high ceiling, the white tiles,
the bathtub with claws.
The boy heard me, but he didn't ask
what was wrong.
              I think you're like him, Anthony,
that you've gone to Florida
with your girlfriend, and Living with Art
was too big to fit in the car
with your summer clothes and sleeping bags
and cassette tapes.

The week I stole your book
my mother asked me which was better,
a lumpectomy or a mastectomy.
              It's about the first thing
she's ever asked me, and I'm 51.
I could see she was leaning
toward the mastectomy
so I said, "Go for it.
Have them take the whole thing."
Why mess around, right, Anthony?

She has a prosthesis now.
Every night she washes it
in liquid Ivory and puts it
in its little cradle

so the oils of her body
            don't eat away at it
before the two years are up
and the insurance people
give her another one.

That's what I call living with art,
the prosthesis in its cradle
            like the shape of a child
in the sculptured arms of its mother,
so smooth I want to touch it,
but when I do, it's cold.

Just Looking

All over New Jersey people are thinking about the shore.
In malls and chill offices they lick their lips for salt.
Walls of honey-colored light press against windows
that cannot open. From inside, people touch
the warmed glass. If they could lie down in the hot sand,
towels on their faces, nothing would hurt.

Birds caged in migration move toward the light.
Clocks blink in them, making their scaled feet dance.
I too have the season in my hollow bones. Restless
as a beach flea, I drive toward the shore, my hair
blown back like cordgrass in the burning wind. I stop
somewhere, a parking lot, and look at the water.

Here a tern stutters in the brackish air. Silverweed
blooms in the salt-marsh hay. With each wave
I hear the sand slipping back. I am learning the language:
the wave's recurrence, the eager fingers of the tide.
I watch the light shine up from the swaying water.

The Woman Who Tries to Believe

Beneath the tin roof of a stone porch a woman
listens. Rain clicks on tin, creating time, minutes
in a row like garnets knotted on a sturdy thread.
She believes a rose turning in its moment

of near perfection does exist apart from its dead self,
the mat of rotted petals like a hole stabbed by crows
in the side of a dead raccoon, crows that remember
and seek the dead heart. When a car passes on the gravel,

their beaks return to the blood before the splashed water
flattens itself. To the woman the rain on the roof
sounds like frogs she hears marking their need
for each other, ticking, awake when she is awake

in the night. Most mornings she lifts a dead frog
from the pool with the rescue hook. In the night,
blue light rising out of the pool charms the frogs
from their muddy slough. She believes they must hurl

themselves in, leaping on gigantic legs, purposeful,
eager, dying already. Everything ends, she knows this,
but she tells herself it happens in a different blue pool,
in a different, less insistent, kind of rain.

Losing the Farm

What we had is gone, the stone porch, bright fall
loading trees with light, the sheep that blundered
through the open door. Beyond a thin wall
an old woman thumped her stick and made me wonder

how much longer she could struggle with the stairs.
In her half of the house the hall clock struck
and struck again. Outside, the sway-backed mare
bent to the grass beside a pock-marked truck.

We were all waiting. Men were cutting trees
in the orchard, dreams that had bloomed,
bouquets of butterflies. Briskly, you shelled peas
and dropped them in a metal bowl. The doomed

farm rode in the sun of its last season.
I swam, alone, up and back, through the blue
water, watching the light, asking the reason
now can never stand against the new.

Angled bones of houses crowded on our hill.
Inside our house your flowers blazed, alive,
crimson and white on every windowsill.
You would not keep the ones that did not thrive.

The Ordinary Destination

Few are ordinary. Those who remain live in small houses,
three steps up to concrete stoops, screen doors from Sears.
They have old couches, tables, children grown and gone.

The ordinary man plans to outlive his dog.
He's done it before, calling the township to pick up the body,
cold on the *Trenton Times*. This knowledge makes him kind.

The dog obeys. She never thinks of death, yet will go gray,
stiffen, make strange noises, smell, and meanwhile, satisfy
by quickly taking small and eager steps toward death.

The ordinary man fears and loves the dark, walking at night,
hearing the neighbors on their porches, smelling the damp weeds,
knowing that this complete, deep, intoxicating breath

could be the end of breathing, or that, as they always do,
he and the dog could turn toward home, watch TV, sleep, and dream,
turning and waking, breathing, both of them, through the night.

Morning on West Street, Pitman

The leaves in a woman's trees touch
companionably while the deep color
of her porch's all-weather carpet
suffuses her, dyes her blue to the bone.

Across the narrow street her neighbor snaps
a TV on, splashing herself with images.
Down the block, men tumble recycling into a truck.
Everywhere the shining wheels and gears

that drive the day turn together. The woman
toes herself back and forth in an old porch swing,
remembers her parents at the kitchen table,
their heavy cups clanking in their saucers,

the Swedish words blurred, but the melody
of their voices steady and complete.
In a street of angles and close spaces
what is it to live in the body?

So much is expected of her as she ages—
to keep up appearances, stay active.
An outside cat yawns by its empty bowls.
The inside cats warm window sills

with their long bodies, submerged in dreams.
The woman rides in the flowing air. Everything
murmurs its expected pattern. What she loves
is West Street, day coming up among the trees.

A Sense of Direction

Houses stand serenely at the rims of perfect squares.
Slants of darkness reach the farthest fields
and cover the dust, the longest shadows in the world.

Lavender stains the air. In the white houses
women are stirring Jell-o, warming the little kitchens
with its sweetness. The news arrives from so far away

it seems a story, a fabulous invention. The radios
switch to music, songs the women remember
from riding in the dark in their boyfriends' cars.

Sewn into the women's bodies is the certainty of north,
of the way west. Near them on the floors, babies
pat the holes they've found in the shining linoleum.

Beyond the darkening windows, reflected rooms
take possession of bare yards. Ghost children play there
till mothers lift them, feed them suppers of air.

Mark on a Mirror

A woman who used to start her days walking
from room to room emptying ash trays
lives now in a single room.

At night, her former house rises around her,
roof bent beneath the drill-marked sky.
People are near, supper in the oven.

Whose dog is this, nosing her stockinged leg?
She wakes from the repeated dream of slanted light
sorting through dust motes by a front window,

of dragging on an insubstantial cigarette.
She remembers a handprint on a mirror, mark
of a child trying to reach into another world.

The moon drops a glamorous silver coat across her bed.
Who will guard the woman's step, secure the clasp
of pearls at the back of her neck, balance her

on the turning ball of the world, her feet
like sweaty sisters in their sheer suits?
Can the moon protect her from blindness,

from staring tirelessly at the sea, the water improbably
forgetful? Will the moon lift her from the trench
of herself, hand her her broken umbrella?

Katie Comes Home

Katie sits where the dark leaves fall, a blanket
around her shoulders. She hears the old whisperings
along the sidewalks, watches lights go out

in the house where she used to live. She cannot
remember the name of the doll she loved,
the one who extended her dignity around her

on the bedroom shelf. The doll did not frown.
Her little indented face had nose holes
and closing eyes with brittle fringes.

Katie had ripped the doll's chest apart, found
her clockwork heart. When she held it in her hand,
she couldn't discover what made it cry.

She envies stones their home in the dirt.
She imagines they shift comfortably like bodies
in bed, their life's work a dark sleep.

She hears a lock click shut nearby. Only
the calculating moon considers the woman
on the paving, opens a shadow behind her.

Tidemark, Atlantic City

for Clarence

An osprey carries a fish in his eager feet,
both heads forward, fish and bird, invisible
air sliding around them. Down in a broken
tree he rips red flesh from a net of bone,
sees you watching but doesn't stop.

Hunger and caution balance the birds—
sharp-tailed sparrows like rodents, furtive
in the weeds, egrets that wait for a stabbing catch.
If you take the car, it's minutes to the city,
the sealed darkness of a casino, the old

in their bright clothes. You ride past a house
where life ebbed out. A boy lived here.
He played a wooden flute. His mother
brought leftover food when nightclubs
closed and day began. Sammy Davis stood

backstage, she said, never sat, kept the crease
in his beautiful clothes. Herons stand
that way—exhibit practiced grace, wait for the glint
of food in turbid water. Then they move so fast
it's like bursting, like throwing your flute

in the bitter sea, watching it kick, take on water,
drown. You wait where the morning tide lifted
its trash so far, no farther. You know what there is—
plastic and sea wrack and dead fish, the smell
of food a drunk pushed back on a shining plate.

Endurance

Bernita married Larry, went to college
and started in on poetry there. She gave me
a picture of herself reading in a bookstore,
showing her bad teeth, eyes almost closed, but hair
glowing, fleets of books backing her up.

Here I am, an arson suspect, she wrote
on the back in green ink. I thought her book
would be green like the poems she brought
to my kitchen, but it's disguised as an ordinary
book, black print, thin white pages.

I found one in the bookstore down the block.
Inside the cover green ink: *May 13, 1991.*
Julie, Some things last. Bernita. I'd go in
every day, past mysteries and horror and death
and dying and its subsection suicide, pull

the soft book from among the others, press
my face against it, feel the extra liquid
in my closed eyes. One day it went home
with someone. I see people working
at computers, the rooms behind them

full of books and light. From the street
I watch a woman stand. She holds clear wine
in one hand, reaches with the other for a book
she will read to a friend. I have my own
at home. *Barb,* it says, *Some things last.*

Chill

Our bodies go ahead of us, first
to the kind of shade the moon makes,
then dust and dissolution. All is forgiven then—
softened flesh, bruised bone.

A freight train whistles through the intersection
by the soybean mill, its sadness unintentional.
I am my age. Everything has a patina.
Is it dust, scum like the smear on a store window

where somebody in another season
sloshed cherry pop? It still looks sweet,
but if I touch it with my tongue,
it will taste bitter. Near me in a crowd

sits a man who loves his wife. It's chilly.
He's keeping her warm. I know that the closer
he holds her, the farther she's gone.
In the failing light his glasses shine like little moons.

Every day has its weather. Today the cirrus clouds
stroked the top of the sky, soft as hair.
Where they are, so high in the atmosphere,
every wisp is a shard of ice.

My Friend, Dead in a Winter Storm

An evil moon stung the side of the world,
driving the tide across the beach and
into the streets. Your shore house stood
among the others like a child waiting
where you said to wait. Against advice

you left lit windows and neat lawns, slid
your car out under huge moving shadows.
All the way to the shore everything howled.
The intricate inner life of your body
was silting up, sand in the vessels that feed

the heart. Your head already lay on the wet lip
of night. You saved the house, fought plywood
into place across its doors and empty eyes.
Rain slashed at your heavy clothes.
Then you screamed, stumbled, clutched

the ribbed vault of your chest, slumped
on the steps. Your hands are so cold.
Now you are ice caves. You are a bell.
You are the ache in my own chest that clangs
down my arms to my despairing hands.

The Weight of What Is Falling

Deer can rise up on single pairs
of legs. Serious, vigilant, they paw
the air like young women teaching poetry,
lifting their arms, almost overbalanced.
Jugglers feel the weight of objects
even as they're falling, before
they must be caught, tossed, caught
again. When the jugglers bow, they cradle
their wooden clubs against their thin chests.
Is your day stippled with anxiety?
At death, your heart cannot be forced
to testify. You will be able to toss it
in the air. A conjurer, you'll make
from it a whistling bird. The loose bag
of your body will let you go. The thorns
on your crown will be open beaks.

Winter Ends

I am the woman who touches your window
with a gloved hand, then turns and walks away.
Dark shapes keep moving by your house, roaring.

They are cars, you see that, but they could turn
into animals that rip the throats from other animals,
then lick their paws repeatedly, spreading their claws

like fingers. I watch a mourning dove flap a wing,
shudder it into place. Soiled snow lies in a shaded angle,
newspapers blown there yellowed by the dirty sun.

Sagging shapes of your body bloat the clothes on the line,
your underwear stained in fading patches. You know
how waves keep turning themselves over, sending

the same garbled message in the salty foam?
Don't worry. This life is more than the body. Grass
suddenly turns green, tips up beside the highway.

Daffodils struggle from the right of way. Rain goes
to the ground, then into the ground the way dreams
travel through your grieving body and then go on.